HISTORY IN WRITING

THE
AMERICAN
REVOLUTION

STEWART ROSS

Evans

Published by Evans Brothers Limited
2A Portman Mansions
Chiltern Street
London
W1U 6NR

© Evans Brothers Limited 2001

First published in 2001
Printed in Grafo, Spain

British Library Cataloguing in Publication Data

Ross, Stewart
    American Revolution
    1.United States - History - Revolution, 1775-1783 -
    Sources - Juvenile literature
    I.Title
    973.3
    ISBN 0237521695

Design – Neil Sayer
Editorial – Nicola Barber
Maps – Tim Smith
Consultant – Marianne S. Wokeck, Associate Professor,
Department of History, Indiana University, Indianapolis
Production – Jenny Mulvanny

Title page picture: Signing the Constitution

To find out more about the American Revolution, try looking
at these websites:

http://www.historyplace.com/unitedstates/revolution

http://www.pbs.org/ktca/liberty/chronicle

http://w3.one.net/~mwelier/ushda/list.htm

http://www.historymatters.gmu.edu/

**http://earlyamerica.com/earlyamerica/milestones/
    index.html**

http://odur.let.rug.nl/~usa/D/#1776

VISIT OUR WEBSITE
Evans
www.evansbooks.co.uk

ACKNOWLEDGEMENTS

For permission to reproduce copyright pictorial material, the author and
publishers gratefully acknowledge the following:

cover: (background image: Declaration of Independence) Peter Newark's
American Pictures (top left: Yorktown): Chateau de Versailles, France/Bridgeman
Art Library (top right: George III) (middle: Virginia currency) (bottom left: stars
and stripes): Peter Newark's American Pictures (bottom right: Boston Tea Party):
Private Collection/Bridgeman Art Library
title page: (signing the Constitution) Hall of Representatives, Washington D.C.,
USA/Bridgeman Art Library
page 7 (top) Peter Newark's American Pictures (bottom) Peter Newark's
American Pictures **page 8** Private Collection/Bridgeman Art Library **page 9** (left)
Mary Evans Picture Library (right) Magdalen College, Oxford/Bridgeman Art
Library **page 10** (top) Bridgeman Art Library (bottom) Bridgeman Art Library
page 13 Peter Newark's American Pictures **page 14** Mary Evans Picture Library
page 15 (top) Peter Newark's American Pictures (middle) Peter Newark's
American Pictures **page 16** Private Collection/Bridgeman Art Library
page 17 (top) Peter Newark's American Pictures (bottom) Philip Mould,
Historical Portraits Ltd, London UK/Bridgeman Art Library **page 18** Peter
Newark's American Pictures **page 19** Mary Evans Picture Library **page 20** (top)
Mary Evans Picture Library (bottom) Peter Newark's American Pictures **page 22**
(top) Mary Evans Picture Library (bottom) Peter Newark's American Pictures
page 23 Mary Evans Picture Library **page 24** Peter Newark's American Pictures
page 25 (top) Peter Newark's American Pictures (middle) Peter Newark's
American Pictures **page 26** Peter Newark's American Pictures **page 27** (top)
Private Collection/Bridgeman Art Library (bottom) Peter Newark's American
Pictures **page 28** (top) Peter Newark's American Pictures (bottom) Private
Collection/Bridgeman Art Library **page 30** Peter Newark's American Pictures
page 31 (top)Peter Newark's American Pictures (bottom) Peter Newark's
American Pictures **page 33** (left) Peter Newark's American Pictures (right) Peter
Newark's American Pictures **page 34** (top) Mary Evans Picture Library (bottom)
Peter Newark's American Pictures **page 35** Peter Newark's American Pictures
page 36 Chateau de Versailles, France/Bridgeman Art Library **page 37** Peter
Newark's American Pictures **page 38** (top) Peter Newark's American Pictures
(bottom) Christie's Images, London, UK/Bridgeman Art Library **page 39**
Bettmann/Corbis **page 40** (left) Peter Newark's American Pictures (right) Private
Collection/Bridgeman Art Library **page 41** Peter Newark's American Pictures
page 42 Peter Newark's American Pictures **page 43** Peter Newark's American
Pictures **page 44** Peter Newark's American Pictures **page 45** Mary Evans
Picture Library **page 46** Hall of Representatives, Washington D.C.,
USA/Bridgeman Art Library **page 47** Peter Newark's American Pictures **page 48**
(top) Peter Newark's American Pictures (bottom) US Library of Congress **page
49** Peter Newark's American Pictures **page 50** (top) Private
Collection/Bridgeman Art Library (bottom) Private Collection/Bridgeman Art
Library **page 51** Peter Newark's American Pictures **page 52** New York Historical
Society, USA/Bridgeman Art Library **page 53** Peter Newark's American Pictures
page 54 Mary Evans Picture Library **page 55** (left) Yale University Art Gallery,
New Haven, CT, USA/Bridgeman Art Library (right) Peter Newark's American
Pictures **page 56** (right) Bristol City Museum and Art Gallery, UK/ Bridgeman Art
Library (bottom) Musée Carnavalet, Paris, France/Roger-Viollet,
Paris/Bridgeman Art Library **page 57** British Library, London, UK/Bridgeman Art
Library **page 58** Peter Newark's American Pictures **page 59** (top) Peter
Newark's American Pictures (bottom) Peter Newark's American Pictures

For permission to reproduce copyright material for the documents, the author
and publisher gratefully acknowledge the following:

page 7 (bottom), **page 33** From America Firsthand, Vol.1 by Robert D. Marus &
David Burner, published by Bedford/St Martins, 1998 **page 13** (bottom), **page
53** From History of the United States of America, by Hugh Brogan, published by
Longman,1985 **page 15** From Foundations of Colonial America: A
Documentary History, by W.Keith Kavenagh, published by Chelsea House, 1973
page 19 From English Historical Documents, Vol. IX, ('American Colonial
Documents to 1776') edited by M. Jensen, published by Routledge, 1955. By
permission of Routledge **page 23, page 25** (top), **page 29** (top), **page 31**
(top), **page 45** (top), **page 49** (bottom), **page 59** (bottom): From Great Issues
in American History: From the Revolution to the Civil War, 1765-1865, by R.
Hofstadter, published by Vintage Books, an imprint of Random House, 1958
page 25: (bottom) From Discovering the American Past: A Look At The Evidence
to 1877 by B. Wheeler and Susan Becker, published in 1986 by Houghton
Mifflin **page 27, page 49** (bottom): From An American History, by Rebecca B.
Gruver, published by Addison Wesley, 1976 **page 35, page 39** From Treaties
and Other International Acts of the United States of America, Vol.2, edited by
Hunter Miller, published by the US Government Printing Office, 1931 **page 43,
page 45** (bottom), Major Problems in the Era of the American Revolution, 1760 –
1791, by Richard D. Brown, published by DC Heath & Co, 1991 **page 57** From
Citizens, by Simon Schama, published by Viking Press, 1989. Reproduced by
permission of Penguin Books Ltd.

While every effort has been made to secure permission to use copyright
material, Evans Brothers apologise for any errors or omissions in the above list
and would be grateful for notification of any corrections to be included in
subsequent editions.

 CONTENTS

CHAPTER 1

ORIGINS
THREE REVOLUTIONS IN ONE

The American Revolution was the process by which Britain's 13 colonies in North America became a separate nation. This was achieved by the end of the war of 1775-83. As a consequence, the phrase 'American Revolution' can be used to mean just the military conflict and the changes that occurred while it was in progress. According to this view, the revolution began with the outbreak of fighting in 1775 and ended with the Peace of Paris in 1783.

An engraving of the Battle of Lexington Green (19 April 1775), the first encounter of the American Revolution. Working more than 50 years after the event, the artist clearly wanted to present the British as the aggressors.

However, America's revolution was more than just a military triumph. It reflected a revolution in thinking that started long before 1775. Nor was the revolution over when the guns fell silent. It took the Americans eight more years to establish a satisfactory form of government. Indeed, it was the American Constitution (1787) and its Bill of Rights (1789) that changed a triumphant uprising into a true revolution.
If the world was surprised by the Americans' successful rebellion, it was eventually transformed by the impact of their Constitution.

The theme of this book, therefore, is that the American Revolution was made up of three overlapping strands. First, there was a change in thinking, both in the American colonies and in Britain, which gave rise to the opinion that people had a right to choose their own form of government (self-determination). One logical conclusion drawn from these new ideas was that people also had the right to free themselves from a government not of their choosing. This part of the revolution happened slowly and in many cases reluctantly. For example, when war broke out it was viewed initially by many Americans, including George Washington (see page 28), more as a civil war than a war of independence.

The second part of the revolution was the war itself; the trial of strength that earned Americans their independence. The last part was the constitutional revolution. This cemented the new thinking and the military victory in a form of government the like of which had never been seen before. Only when the Bill of Rights became law in 1791 was the full American Revolution finally over.

George Washington (1732-99) was the general who masterminded American victory in the war of 1775-83.

REVOLUTION

Political revolution is rapid, large-scale and permanent political upheaval. The idea originated in Ancient Greece. The Greek philosophers Plato and Aristotle believed that revolutions were destructive because rapid change was bound to be badly thought out. Fear of revolution continued in medieval thinking, too. But from the Renaissance onwards, attitudes changed. Thinkers such as the English poet John Milton (above) and the German philosopher Immanuel Kant suggested that revolution was progressive, allowing freedom to replace tyranny. This was the view of the majority of Americans who took up arms against the British crown.

The war that turned the revolution in thinking into a revolution in fact began on 19 April 1775. British troops going from Boston to Concord, Massachusetts, encountered armed resistance at Lexington. Fighting broke out. Later, the Massachusetts assembly gave its account of what happened. Realising how important it was to get public opinion on its side, it blamed the British for starting the conflict.

The Americans who had mustered.

Mustered means 'gathered together'.

This means the British troops.

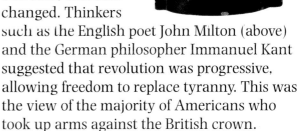

The town of Lexington... was alarmed, and a company of the inhabitants mustered on the occasion... the regular troops on their way to Concord marched into the said town of Lexington, and the said company, on their approach, began to disperse; notwithstanding this, the regulars rushed on with great violence, and first began hostilities by firing on said Lexington Company whereby they killed eight and wounded several others... the regulars continued to fire until those of the said company who were neither killed nor wounded had made their escape.

THE ENGLISH REVOLUTION

The roots of the American Revolution stretch back to the English Revolution of the 17th century. In 1600, political power in England rested with the monarch and the parliament. The king or queen and his or her chosen ministers made all important policy decisions. The monarch was also 'supreme governor' of England's Protestant church, the Church of England.

The monarch was limited by a tradition that he or she could raise taxes only with the consent of parliament. Parliament consisted of the House of Lords, made up of nobles and bishops of the Church of England, and the House of Commons. Members of the Commons (MPs) were elected from the towns and counties by the 'political nation' – men of wealth and standing. As monarchs were always short of money, they needed the support of the Commons to rule effectively.

The system worked reasonably well under James I (reigned 1603-25), the time when England's first American colonies were founded. But his son Charles I (reigned 1625-49) alienated the political nation by a series of ill-considered policies. The two sides drifted further apart and finally went to war. Parliament (largely the House of Commons) won the English Civil War (1642-5), executed Charles I (1649) and declared the country a Republic.

The Republic, led by Oliver Cromwell, failed to find a balance between the powers of parliament and those of the head of the government. It also angered the political nation by abolishing the Church of

Oliver Cromwell (1599-1658)

England. In 1660 the old system of government, under Charles II, was restored. Nonetheless, the tension between monarch and parliament remained.

When Charles' Roman Catholic brother, James II (reigned 1685-8), tried to give the crown absolute power, the

A contemporary painting of the execution of King Charles I in 1649. The event sent shockwaves of horror throughout Europe and divided the American colonists.

political nation deserted him. In the Glorious Revolution (1688-9), James' daughter Mary and her husband William accepted parliament's invitation to become king and queen (Mary II and William III). James II fled to France.

The balance of power between the monarch and parliament had now swung permanently in favour of parliament. Parliament controlled taxes and expenditure. The monarch was still nominally head of the government, but had to appoint ministers who had the approval of parliament.

The English Revolution established the principle that the people – at least those with economic power – had the right to choose a government that acted in their interests. It was a principle that Americans would embrace warmly in the next century.

THE CHURCH OF ENGLAND

King Henry VIII (reigned 1509-47) set up the Church of England when he renounced the authority of the pope and put himself at the head of the Church. Henry's daughter, Queen Elizabeth I (reigned 1558-1603), re-established the Church as a Protestant organisation that retained aspects of Roman Catholicism. But many Protestants wished to 'purify' the Church of these remnants of Roman Catholicism. These opponents of the Church of England were known as Puritans. Some of them, dissatisfied with the religious state of affairs in England, emigrated to New England to found what they hoped would be a more godly society.

After its victory in the English Civil War, the parliamentary army held a series of debates on how the country should be governed. The most radical contribution came from a common soldier, Rainborough, who argued that everyone had a right to choose the government. His view is not unlike that put forward by many Americans at the time of the revolution (see page 31).

He means 'man'.

Here **as** means 'just as'.

Rainborough: I really think that the poorest he that is in England hath a life to live, as the greatest he; and therefore truly... I think that every man that is to live under a government ought first by his own counsel put himself under that government.

Counsel means 'choice'.

As the English political nation believed it had a right to be represented in parliament, it could hardly argue that fellow countrymen living in America did not share that right. Here, the English writer Soame Jenyns argued that Americans were indeed represented in parliament.

These were expanding industrial centres which had no MPs.

Many great names are quoted to prove that every Englishman, whether he has a right to vote for a representative or not, is still represented in the British Parliament... But then I will ask one question: Why does not this imaginary representation extend to America?... If the towns of Manchester and Birmingham, sending no representatives to parliament, are notwithstanding there represented, why are not the cities of Albany and Boston equally represented in that assembly? Are they not alike British subjects?....

Notwithstanding means 'nevertheless'.

THE THIRTEEN COLONIES

In 1497 John Cabot reached Newfoundland, Canada, and claimed North America for the English crown. It took another 250 years for this claim to become a reality.

Spaniards established the first European settlement in North America at St Augustine, Florida, in 1565. In 1608 the French founded Quebec, Canada, and six years later Dutch fur traders built a trading post at Albany, New York. Meanwhile, in 1607 the English had settled Jamestown, Virginia. After difficult beginnings, the colony prospered. By 1619 it organised an assembly to discuss common problems. Thus the principle of people having a say in their own government moved from England to the 'New World'.

The New England colonies began the following year when the *Mayflower* pilgrims settled at Plymouth. In 1691 Plymouth became part of another Puritan colony, Massachusetts (founded in 1630). By 1636, permanent settlements also existed in New Hampshire, Connecticut and Rhode Island.

Maryland, founded in 1634, established another principle of colonial life when it passed an act of religious toleration (1649). In 1664 Delaware, New York and New Jersey were added to England's growing North American empire, and in 1730 North and South Carolina (founded in 1653 and 1670) became individual colonies. Quakers settled in Pennsylvania in 1681 and James Oglethorpe founded Georgia, the last of the 13 colonies, in 1733.

Around the English colonies stretched an arc of French settlements in Canada, on the shores of the Great Lakes and along the Mississippi Valley. Their presence drew the English colonies together. Not until the decisive French and Indian War of 1754-63 (which became part of Europe's Seven Years' War, see pages 16-17) was the French threat finally removed.

Two other important groups complete the picture of North America in the mid 18th century. Native Americans, largely driven from their lands in the east, still inhabited the vast unmapped

EUROPEAN SETTLEMENT OF NORTH AMERICA IN THE 17TH AND 18TH CENTURIES

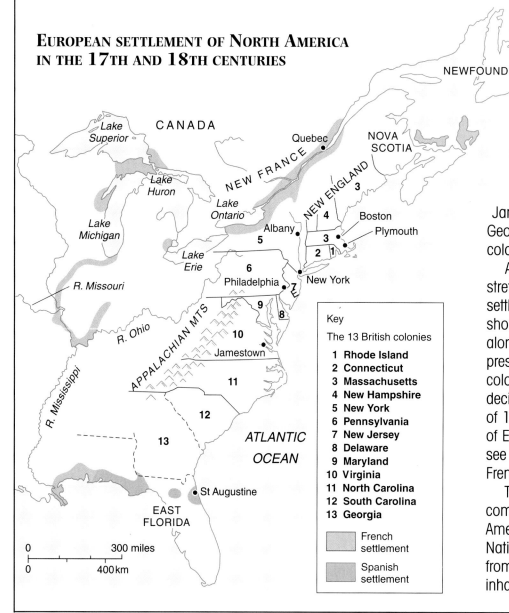

Key

The 13 British colonies

1 Rhode Island
2 Connecticut
3 Massachusetts
4 New Hampshire
5 New York
6 Pennsylvania
7 New Jersey
8 Delaware
9 Maryland
10 Virginia
11 North Carolina
12 South Carolina
13 Georgia

French settlement

Spanish settlement

territories of the West. The only interest they had in English-French or English-American squabbles was if one side undertook to leave them in peace. The second group was black slaves imported from Africa since 1619. In 1770 there were half a million slaves in British North America, around 20 per cent of the total population. Questions of empire were largely irrelevant to them unless, of course, white Americans were prepared to offer them the same freedoms as they sought for themselves.

The Pilgrim Fathers were the English Puritans who sailed to the 'New World' on the *Mayflower*. They landed in December 1620. This picture shows a romanticised view of their landfall. In reality, after weeks at sea, the thin and exhausted settlers would have been dressed in shabby clothes.

This description of the first sighting of Europeans by Native Americans was written down in the mid 18th century. It refers to the arrival off Manhattan of the ship of the English explorer Henry Hudson in 1609.

Indians is an old-fashioned term for 'Native Americans'.

A long time ago, when there was no such thing known to the Indians as people with a white skin, some Indians who had been out fishing, and where the sea widens, espied at a great distance something remarkably large swimming, or floating on the water, and such as they had never seen before. They immediately returning to the shore, appraised their countrymen of what they had seen and pressed them to go out with them and discover what it might be. These together hurried out, and saw to their great surprise the phenomenon, but could not agree what it might be; some concluding it either to be an uncommon large fish, or other animal, while others were of the opinion it must be some very large house.

Appraised means 'told'.

Speaking at the Stamp Act Congress of 1765 (see page 22), the South Carolina delegate Christopher Gadsden put into words what had been going through American minds for some time. While referring to their English descent, he believed all colonials should now begin thinking of themselves as belonging to a single nation – America.

Inherent means 'fixed'.

We should all endeavour to stand upon the broad and common ground of those natural and inherent rights that we all feel and know, as men and as descendants of Englishmen, we have a right to... There ought to be no New England men, no New Yorker, etc. known on the continent, but all of us Americans.

BRITAIN'S IMPERIAL TRIUMPH

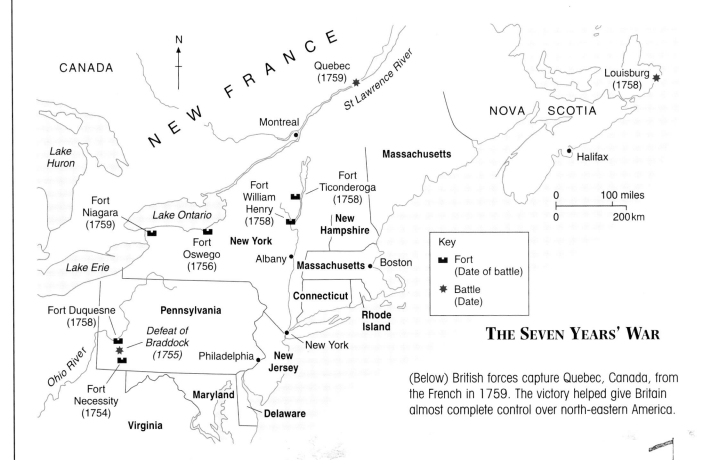

CANADA

N

NEW FRANCE

Quebec
(1759) ✴

St Lawrence River

Louisburg
(1758) ✴

NOVA SCOTIA

Lake
Huron

Montreal

Massachusetts

Halifax

Fort
Niagara
(1759)

Lake Ontario

Fort
William
Henry
(1758)

Fort
Ticonderoga
(1758)

New
Hampshire

Fort
Oswego
(1756)

New York

Albany

Massachusetts • Boston

Lake Erie

Connecticut

Fort Duquesne
(1758)

Pennsylvania

Rhode
Island

Defeat of
Braddock
(1755)

New York

Ohio River

Philadelphia

New
Jersey

Fort
Necessity
(1754)

Maryland

Delaware

Virginia

0   100 miles
0   200 km

Key

🔳 Fort
(Date of battle)

✴ Battle
(Date)

THE SEVEN YEARS' WAR

(Below) British forces capture Quebec, Canada, from the French in 1759. The victory helped give Britain almost complete control over north-eastern America.

A glance at the map on page 12 shows that in 1756 Britain was not the only colonial power in North America. Spain held Florida, while France controlled Canada and was seeking to extend its power south along the Ohio and Mississippi rivers to New Orleans. While Spain's days of greatness were gone, both Britain and France dreamed of controlling the entire North American continent.

The issue was resolved by war. The conflict known in America as the French and Indian War (1754-63) and in Europe as the Seven Years' War (1756-63) was fought in both Europe and North America. British strategy, masterminded by the prime minister William Pitt, was to allow Britain's ally Prussia to attack France in Europe, while Britain and its American colonial allies fought the French in North America.

The outcome was not a foregone conclusion. Although outnumbered, France's American forces were better organised, trained and equipped than those of their enemies. They were also adept at forging alliances with

the Native Americans. In 1754, before the outbreak of war in Europe, the colonial commander George Washington was driven from Fort Necessity (between Maryland and the River Ohio) by French forces. A year later, the English general Edward Braddock suffered a devastating defeat at River Monongahela. The French went on to capture Fort Oswego in 1756 and Fort William Henry in 1757.

In 1758, boosted by reinforcements from Europe, the British began to gain the upper hand. After failing to take Fort Ticonderoga, they seized Louisburg, Quebec (1759) and Montreal (1760), leaving them in control of eastern North America. This was confirmed at the Treaty of Paris (1763) at which the British gained Canada and all the land between the River Mississippi and the eastern coastline.

However, Britain's triumph was a costly one. During the war the national debt had almost doubled to £170 million. Moreover, the British commander in North America, General Jeffrey Amherst, estimated that the substantial garrisons needed in North America to maintain the frontier and keep control over the newly acquired territories would cost in excess of £300,000 a year. Where would the money come from? One obvious source was from the colonies themselves.

NATIVE TRAGEDY

Britain's victory was a disaster for the Ottawa, Huron, Chippewa and other native peoples of the northeast. For a while, they had preserved a degree of independence by siding with France against Britain. Most had changed sides by 1759, lured by the promise that they would be left in peace after the war.

When the promise proved false, the Ottawa chief Pontiac launched a long and ultimately disastrous war (1763-6) against the new masters of his territories.

Pontiac, the Ottawa chief who led the unsuccessful revolt against the British in 1763

The English philosopher, John Locke (1632-1704)

In the 1680s, the philosopher John Locke argued that the only valid government was one to which the people had given their consent. Later, this argument was used by Americans opposed to paying taxes levied by the British parliament.

The **legislative** means 'parliament'

For example, laws authorising the raising of taxes.

Americans had no representatives in the British Parliament.

The constitution of the legislative is the first and fundamental act of society... by the consent and appointment of the people, without which no one man, or number of men, amongst them can have authority of making laws... that shall be binding to the rest. When any one, or more, shall take upon them to make laws whom the people have not appointed so to do, they make laws without authority, which the people are not therefore bound to obey.

PROCLAMATION AND PINE

THE PROCLAMATION OF 1763

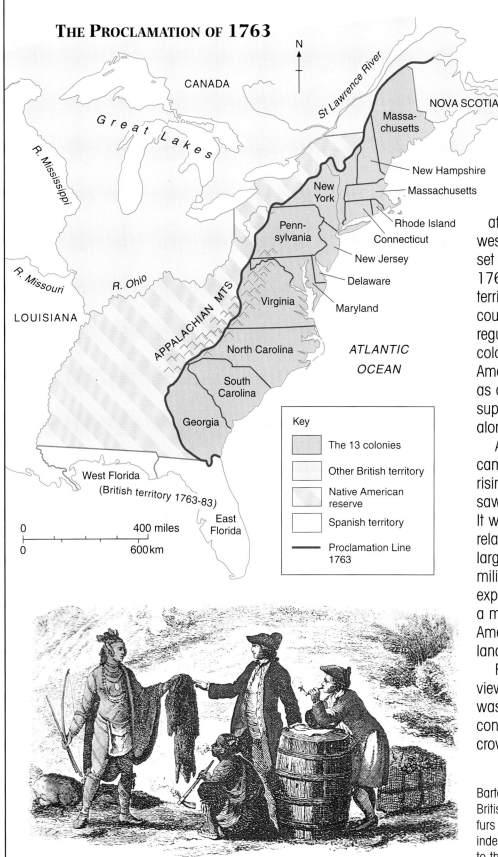

N

CANADA

Great Lakes

R. Mississippi

R. Missouri

R. Ohio

LOUISIANA

APPALACHIAN MTS

St Lawrence River

NOVA SCOTIA

Massa-chusetts

New Hampshire

New York

Massachusetts

Penn-sylvania

Rhode Island

Connecticut

New Jersey

Delaware

Virginia

Maryland

North Carolina

ATLANTIC OCEAN

South Carolina

Georgia

West Florida
(British territory 1763-83)

East Florida

| 0 | 400 miles |
| 0 | 600 km |

Key

- The 13 colonies
- Other British territory
- Native American reserve
- Spanish territory
- —— Proclamation Line 1763

Many colonies had grievances against the British government which made them look unfavourably on requests for financial assistance. The issue that caused the greatest irritation was Britain's attempt to regulate the colonies' western frontier. The policy was set out in a royal proclamation of 1763 that limited the western territory into which the colonists could move. It also attempted to regulate trade between the colonists and the Native Americans. Royal officers (known as commissioners) were to supervise all trade beyond a line along the Appalachian Mountains.

Although the proclamation came too late to stop the Pontiac rising (see box page 17), London saw it as a reasonable document. It wished to maintain peaceful relations with Native Americans largely for financial relations – military confrontation was expensive. It also believed it had a moral duty to protect Native Americans from the aggression of land-hungry colonials.

From an American point of view, however, the proclamation was unreasonable. By handing control of the West to the British crown, it reduced the power of

Bartering for furs. To the irritation of the British government, the profitable trade in furs drew American colonists into making independent treaties with Native Americans to the west of the Appalachian Mountains.

colonial governments. It also upset settlers who hoped to make their fortunes in the West. They condemned the proclamation as an oppressive measure imposed by an alien government.

Americans were also worried by the existence of a British army in North America after the end of the war. London said it was needed to secure the western frontier. The colonists believed it was an insult to local forces. Moreover, like many Englishmen, they associated a standing (permanent) army with tyrannous government, such as the one in France.

The issue of the proclamation and standing army touched all the colonies more or less alike. More local annoyances added to the feeling of discontent. The Church of England (see page 11) had few supporters in New England. New Englanders, therefore, were angered when Archbishop of Canterbury Thomas Secker favoured the Church of England over other Protestant churches, such as the Congregationalists (see box). For example, he banned Congregationalist missionary work among the Native Americans. Pennsylvania, New Jersey and New York grumbled over the British government's power (abandoned in England long ago) to dismiss their judges when it wished. New Hampshire, Massachusetts and Connecticut resented the White Pine Acts which said that Royal Naval shipbuilders could use all white pine trees not growing on private property. And South Carolina was roused by a quarrel between its elected assembly and its dim-witted governor, who was appointed by the crown.

BISHOPS IN AMERICA

The wide range of Christian beliefs held by the settlers in America ensured that religious toleration became a way of life in most colonies. Successive Archbishops of Canterbury recognised this and resisted the temptation to try and install Anglican bishops even in nominally Anglican colonies such as Virginia. Archbishop Secker opposed this policy. This fuelled American mistrust of Britain's Anglican government, of which he was a part.

The insensitive behaviour of Thomas Secker (1693-1768), Archbishop of Canterbury and head of the Anglican church, irritated New England Protestants at a time when Britain's colonial rule was attracting rising criticism.

George III's Proclamation of 7 October 1763 showed a concern for the welfare of Native Americans that was lacking in the colonies themselves.

Dominion means 'direct control'.

This means all lands to the west of the Appalachian Mountains.

And whereas it is just and reasonable, and essential to our interest, and the security of our colonies, that the several nations or tribes of Indians with whom we are connected, and who live under our protection, should not be molested or disturbed... We do... declare it to be our royal will and pleasure... to reserve under our sovereignty, protection, and dominion, for the use of the said Indians, all the Lands and Territories not included within the limits of our said three new governments...

SEEDS OF REVOLUTION

George Grenville (1712-70) was the British prime minister whose tax-raising measures led to a significant rise in tension between Britain and its American colonies.

British revenue officers deal with smugglers who are attempting to import goods into North America without paying duty.

Britain's parliamentary system of government was representative of the wealthier classes, who also paid the bulk of the taxes. As the tax burden was higher than ever before, the prime minister George Grenville decided to look for new sources of income.

The British had always seen their colonies as primarily commercial ventures. During the 17th century, parliament had passed several Navigation Acts to regulate and maximise the profits from colonial trade. Colonial imports had to be carried in English- or colonial-built ships that were English-owned and manned. 'Enumerated articles' such as tobacco, dyes and sugar shipped between colonies or between Europe and the colonies had to pass through an English port or pay heavy duties. In America, English-controlled customs houses and law courts operated by the Royal Navy were responsible for enforcing the Acts.

During the Seven Years' War, to stop illegal colonial trade with the French, Pitt instructed the Royal Navy to implement the Navigation Acts rigorously. Smugglers were hunted down and corrupt officials prosecuted. The British government found this new severity brought in extra revenue. So, although he knew it would be unpopular, Grenville maintained the Acts after the war. He extended them, too, with a Sugar Act (1764) that reduced the duty on imported foreign molasses but imposed a high duty on refined sugar and banned the import of foreign rum. A Currency Act (1764) banned colonial paper money because much of it was completely worthless.

The Americans, accustomed to light taxation and minimal government, deeply resented Grenville's measures. Colonial businesses that had done well out of the war, such as suppliers to the armed forces, struggled when peace was made. Grenville's legislation made things worse for them. It also raised serious questions of principle. At this stage very few Americans questioned Britain's right to control the colonies,

but many had serious worries about how that control was exercised.

The Admiralty Courts appeared to ignore the basic rights accorded to English citizens – the accused was presumed guilty, and the case was not heard by a jury. And the economic measures looked alarmingly like taxation disguised as trade regulation. In New England – particularly in Boston and Newport – community leaders stirred up resistance and planned a boycott of British goods. Quite suddenly, the Atlantic was starting to look more like a frontier than a highway.

A MATTER OF PRINCIPLE

Prime Minister George Grenville, an able but unimaginative administrator, believed that British MPs represented the colonies 'virtually' (indirectly) in Parliament. He claimed that this gave him the right to tax Americans by laws passed in London. Once Parliament had accepted this principle, the majority of MPs were too proud to back down. As Americans were equally convinced that they were not represented in Parliament, virtually or otherwise, the stage was set for inevitable conflict.

The first Navigation Act was passed in 1651, less than two years after England had become a republic (see page 10). **This section of the Act insists that all English trade be carried in English ships.**

This refers to the remaining members of the Long Parliament that first met in 1640.

For the increase of shipping and the encouragement of the navigation of this nation... be it enacted by this **present Parliament**... that... no goods or commodities whatsoever of the growth, production or manufacture of Asia, Africa or America... as well of the **English plantations** as others, shall be imported or brought into this **Commonwealth** of England, or into Ireland, or any other lands... to this Commonwealth belonging... in any other ship or ships... whatsoever, but only in such as do truly and without fraud belong only to the people of this Commonwealth.

This means 'colonies'.

Commonwealth means 'community'.

In a speech of 1761, Massachusetts lawyer James Otis (1725-83) challenged the British government's right to issue search warrants (Writs of Assistance) to enforce the Navigation Acts. He was one of the first Americans to base his resistance on the principle of natural law. This said that the law beyond human control gave everyone basic rights.

I take this opportunity to declare that whether under a fee or not... I will to my dying day oppose, with all the powers and faculties God has given me, all such instruments of slavery on the one hand and villainy on the other as this Writ of Assistance is... It appears to me the worst instrument of **arbitrary** power, the most destructive of **English liberty** and the fundamental **principles of law**, that ever was found in an English law-book.

Arbitrary means 'unregulated'.

Otis, like almost all Americans, regarded himself as English.

This means the 'natural law'.

NO TAXATION WITHOUT REPRESENTATION

Grenville reckoned that the Sugar Act (see page 20) and other measures would bring in about £45,000 a year. As this was less than the cost of maintaining the North American garrisons, he also introduced an American Stamp Duty Act.

Stamp Duty meant printing all legal and official papers, newspapers, pamphlets and playing cards on paper carrying an embossed stamp. This paper could be bought only from stamp commissioners. It was manufactured in England, where a similar tax had proved efficient and easily collected.

An example of the type of stamp, embossed on British-made paper, which most legal and printed documents had to carry.

This is the first page of the notorious Stamp Act, passed by the British parliament early in 1765.

The Stamp Act became law on 22 March 1765. Grenville's previous measures had doubled the tax Americans paid to Britain. The Stamp Act threatened to double it again. Because duty was payable on shipping documents, it struck where America was most sensitive – trade. Furthermore, it directly affected some influential people in colonial society: lawyers, merchants and journalists.

The Stamp Act was Parliament's first attempt to tax the colonies directly rather than through trade regulation. It produced a ferocious storm of protest. Under the banner 'no taxation without representation', mobs took to the streets in Boston, New York and other large towns. Distributors of Stamps were forced to step down. While most legal business ground to a halt, the proposed boycott of British goods (see page 21) came closer to reality.

The Stamp Act was condemned in pamphlets, letters, newspapers, local meetings and assemblies. On 7 October 1765, delegates from nine colonies met in New York to discuss the situation. This Stamp Act Congress denounced the Act as a violation of their right to be taxed only through their elected representatives. The resolutions of this Congress were significant: for the first time America was speaking with one voice.

Traditionally, reaction to the Stamp Act was seen as Americans starting to think of themselves as a separate nation. The term 'Patriots' for those who opposed the Act reinforces this view. However, many 20th-century historians believe that some popular uprisings were aimed more at wealthy colonials than the British. The mobs attracted the most deprived people in colonial society: unskilled workers, sailors, unemployed and, most deprived of all, African Americans.

KING GEORGE III (REIGNED 1760-1815)

George III (right) tested to the full the balance between royal and parliamentary power established by the Glorious Revolution (1688-9) (see page 11). He was narrow-minded, certain that he was right in all things, and he tried to influence affairs more than was feasible or prudent. This led to his being blamed for errors that were not always of his own making. His determination never to surrender to colonial demands persuaded many Americans that he was the principal cause of the Anglo-American breakdown.

Esteem means 'regard'.

Although the Stamp Act crisis is sometimes said to mark the beginning of the American Revolution, the language adopted by the 1765 Congress in the preface to its Stamp Act Resolutions of 19 October was a model of propriety.

The members of this Congress, sincerely devoted, with the warmest sentiments of affection and duty to His Majesty's Person and Government... **esteem** it our indispensable duty to make the following declarations of our humble opinion...
That His Majesty's... subjects in these colonies, are entitled to all the... rights and liberties of his... subjects within the kingdom of Great-Britain.
That it is inseparably essential to the freedom of a people, and the undoubted right of Englishmen, that no taxes be imposed on them, but with their own consent... or by their representatives.
That the people of these colonies are not, and from their local circumstances cannot be, represented in the House of Commons in Great-Britain.

The House of Commons.

Erroneous means 'false'.

Sympathy for the American cause was strong in many parts of British society. Indeed, the colonists had no firmer supporter in their opposition to the Stamp Act than William Pitt, the prime minister who had masterminded victory in the wars of 1754-63.

I beg leave to tell the **House**... my opinion. It is that the Stamp Act be repealed absolutely ... [for] it was founded on an **erroneous** principle. At the same time, let the sovereign authority of this country over the colonies be asserted in as strong terms as can be devised... that we may... exercise every power whatsoever – except that of taking money out of their pockets without their consent.

FIRST BLOOD

The trade boycott organised by the anti-Stamp Act movement alarmed British merchants. The anxiety spread to Parliament, where the situation was saved by a change of government. In July 1765, George III replaced Grenville with the Marquis of Rockingham. Under pressure from his supporters, Rockingham repealed the Stamp Act and reduced the duty on molasses. However, he also introduced a Declaratory Act stating that Parliament kept control over the colonies 'in all cases whatsoever'. In other words, Parliament insisted it had the right to tax the colonies as and when it saw fit.

Most Americans ignored the Declaratory Act and greeted the repeal of the Stamp Act with great rejoicing. In 1766, a new Chancellor of the Exchequer, Charles Townshend, introduced import duties on necessities such as lead, glass, paint, paper and tea to pay for the American garrisons. The revenue from these taxes was earmarked for official salaries as well as defence. Other measures confirmed that writs of assistance (see page 21) were legal, established new anti-smuggling institutions, and created a Secretary of State for America (1768).

After a period of relative quiet, Philadelphia lawyer John Dickinson alerted Americans to the dangers of Townshend's measures. He objected to all revenue-raising taxation issuing from London. He also said that assemblies would be powerless if they lost the right to grant (or withhold) official salaries.

The protests started over again. 'Sons of Liberty' (radical and sometimes violent groups that had first appeared during the anti-Stamp Act demonstrations) harassed officials and co-ordinated resistance. Assemblies drafted petitions and circulated letters of complaint, for which they were closed. A policy of 'nonimportation' – refusing to import a range of British goods – spread through the colonies. This brought women into the Patriot movement. They banned tea drinking in their households and took to their looms to make good the shortfall in imported woollen and linen cloth.

In 1768, following a serious riot, four regiments of British troops were stationed in Boston. Relations between the Patriots and the soldiers were calm enough at first. Then, on 5 March 1770, a mob of unemployed labourers began pelting a customs house guard with snowballs and oyster shells. In the confusion that followed the soldiers opened fire. Five Patriots, including the African-American Crispus Attucks, were killed. The 'Boston massacre' had given the American cause its first martyrs.

Riot becomes a massacre: this early American engraving of the 'Boston massacre' helped to establish it in American minds as an act of ruthless suppression.

John Dickinson expressed his views in lively articles entitled *Letters from a Farmer in Pennsylvania*. Widely circulated, they played a key role in uniting the colonies behind the Patriot position. At this stage, however, independence from Britain remained an almost unthinkable last resort.

Here then, my dear country men ROUSE yourselves, and behold the ruin hanging over your heads. If you ONCE admit, that Great Britain may lay duties upon her exportations to us, for the purpose of levying money on us only... the tragedy of American liberty is finished... If Great-Britain can order us to come to her for necessaries we want, and can order us to pay what taxes she pleases... we are as abject slaves as France and Poland can show in wooden shoes, and with uncombed hair.

John Dickinson (1732-1808), the pamphleteer who caught the spirit of the American people.

Abject means 'defenceless'.

Both countries were regarded as tyrannies.

Examples of obvious signs of poverty.

SAMUEL ADAMS (1722-1803)

Samuel Adams, a strict Calvinist, ex-tax collector and member of the Massachusetts assembly to 1774, was undoubtedly the most effective of the Patriot leaders at this time. He was at the forefront of opposition to the Stamp Act and the nonimportation movement. Nevertheless, he was a very conservative man and until 1776 refused to accept independence as the remedy to America's problems.

Samuel Adams, the organiser of the celebrated Boston Tea Party (1773) (see page 27).

In the trial for murder that followed the 'Boston massacre', the soldiers' commander, Captain Thomas Preston, gave the following evidence. He was represented in court by the Patriot and future president John Adams, and acquitted.

One of the soldiers having received a severe blow with a stick, stepped a little to one side and instantly fired... On this a general attack was made on the men by a great number of heavy clubs and snowballs... by which all our lives were in imminent danger... Instantly three or four of the soldiers fired... On my asking the soldiers why they fired without orders, they said they heard the word 'fire' and supposed it came from me. This might be the case as many of the mob called out 'Fire! Fire!' But I assured the men that I gave no such order, that my words were, 'Don't fire! Stop your firing!'

OVER THE EDGE

On the day of the 'Boston massacre', Britain's new prime minister, Lord North, announced that all the Townshend duties except that on tea were to be withdrawn. This climb-down and a more relaxed policy on westward expansion soothed American nerves and the nonimportation movement fizzled out.

However, the fundamental differences between Britain and its colonies remained, and Patriots such as Samuel Adams (see page 25) continued to be deeply suspicious. Tension returned in 1772 when Rhode Island smugglers burned HMS *Gaspee*, an anti-smuggling patrol vessel. Rumours circulated that the crown planned to pay some colonial officials directly. This would reduce the power of colonial assemblies, who voted on official salaries and therefore had some control over office holders. In response, a network of inter-colonial corresponding societies was established. Through them, colonial leaders kept in touch and co-ordinated opposition to unpopular government policies.

In 1773, Lord North introduced a Tea Act. This was an attempt to reduce smuggling by allowing the East India Company to sell duty-paid tea at a price below that charged by smugglers. The Sons of Liberty denounced this as a plot to ruin colonial merchants (smugglers and wholesalers) and seduce Americans into paying duty on their favourite drink. Consequently, in December, Samuel Adams organised a band of Bostonians to dress as Native Americans and dump some £10,000 worth of duty-paid tea into Boston harbour.

The exasperated British government responded with five laws (the 'Intolerable Acts') that closed the port of Boston, altered the town's charter in favour of the governor, extended quartering, and strengthened direct royal government. In response, in September 1774 delegates from all the colonies except Georgia gathered in Philadelphia for a Continental Congress. They agreed to support an embargo of British goods, cutting trade with Britain. The more radical delegates talked of America being a separate state under the Crown and therefore not subject to Parliament. A few even spoke of independence.

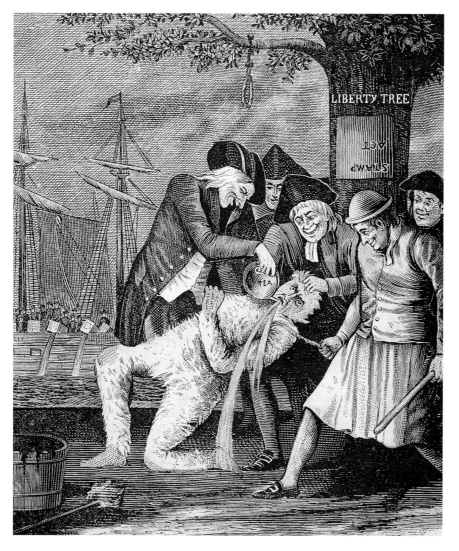

This 1774 cartoon shows a tax collector (who has been 'tarred and feathered' – a popular public humiliation) being forced to drink British tea. In the background the Stamp Act is pinned upside-down to a Liberty Tree.

Fearing a military response from Britain, a few colonial leaders (mostly in Massachusetts) gathered weapons and organised volunteers into a militia (citizen army). The inevitable armed clash finally came on 19 April 1775. British troops went to investigate reports of an arms store at Concord, Massachusetts. Alerted by Paul Revere, local militiamen skirmished with the British at Lexington Green, Concord and along the Concord-Boston road. By nightfall the British had suffered 273 casualties and the Americans 92. The war had begun.

THE BOSTON TEA PARTY

Much of the East India Company tea that arrived in America in 1773 remained on board ship or locked away in customs houses. But Governor Hutchinson of Massachusetts was determined to see the Boston consignment unloaded and sold. The result was the Boston Tea Party, when 342 tea chests were smashed open and their contents scattered on the water. The calculated gesture of defiance horrified moderate colonials. It prompted the Intolerable Acts and was an important step on the road to war.

The Boston Tea Party was a planned act of rebellion that was quickly heralded as spontaneous defiance.

Only over the last 40 years has the significant contribution of American women to the revolutionary movement been recognised. They made nonimportation possible by labouring to produce goods and materials that had previously been imported. Moreover, as this letter from a nameless woman of Philadelphia shows, many were as fervent as the menfolk in their determination not to submit to British 'slavery'.

An American stocking-maker. To support the revolution, American women undertook to manufacture goods that had previously been imported from Britain.

Most luxury goods were imported from Britain.

Actuates means 'moves'.

Niccolo **Machiavelli** was an influential Italian political thinker at the time of the Renaissance.

I know this – that as free I can die but once, but as a slave I shall not be worthy of life. I have the pleasure to assure you that these are the sentiments of all my sister Americans. They have sacrificed assemblies, parties of pleasure, tea drinking and finery, to that great spirit of patriotism that actuates all degrees of people throughout this extensive continent... You say you are no politician. Oh sir, it requires no Machiavellian head to discover this tyranny and oppression. It is written with a sunbeam.

COMMON SENSE

Thomas Paine, a recent immigrant from England, expressed what the majority of Americans were thinking. His pamphlet *Common Sense* (January 1776) was savage. It said that George III was a 'Royal Brute' and God was the true king of America; the struggle was not about 'a few vile acts', but about full independence; British 'corruption' was poisoning the New World.

Few pieces of writing have had such an immediate impact. *Common Sense* was quoted from pulpits, discussed round campfires and read in parlours all over America. It reminded the colonists why they had embarked on their great enterprise and where they were headed. Its delighted reception killed all hope of compromise with Britain.

The defiant mood spread from the provinces to the government in the Continental Congress. Orders went out to attack British shipping, open American ports to merchants from other nations and, for the duration of the crisis, ban the import of slaves. The acceptance of Congress' authority was a crucial development towards nationhood. So were local developments. Assemblies that had not already done so were transforming themselves from colonies into states.

Meanwhile, influential voices in the states and Congress were echoing Paine's call for a formal justification of American action. In June 1776, Congress established a committee to draw up the necessary document. Its five members were John Adams (Massachusetts), Benjamin Franklin (Pennsylvania), Roger Sherman (Connecticut) Robert R. Livingston (New York) and Thomas Jefferson (Virginia). They proved to be some of the wisest and sharpest minds ever assembled.

Congress pruned the committee's document, written by the young Thomas Jefferson, and adopted it on 4 July. In America and elsewhere the day is justly remembered as a landmark in the history of democracy. The first part of the Declaration of Independence, which justified rebellion against a government that denied natural rights, set out the principles upon which all subsequent democratic governments have been

The five-man committee that drew up the Declaration of Independence offers their document to John Hancock, president of the Continental Congress, to inscribe the first signature.

established. The ideas, many drawn from John Locke, were not new, but never before had they been expressed with such clarity.

The second part of the Declaration owed much to Paine's propaganda. It listed Britain's crimes and laid them all at the feet of George III. Parliament did not get a mention. Jefferson knew that rebellion against a tyrant would attract far more sympathy than rebellion against an institution.

THOMAS PAINE (1737-1809)

Born in Norfolk, England, Thomas Paine (below) spent his early adult life working as a corset-maker, sailor, schoolmaster and tax collector. In 1774 he met Benjamin Franklin, who helped him emigrate to Philadelphia. Here, working as a radical journalist, he wrote *Common Sense*. He continued agitating for radical causes for the rest of his life. His avowed atheism eventually alienated most of his supporters and he died in poverty on the farm that grateful New Yorkers had given him many years before.

Jefferson said that in writing the Declaration of Independence he had tried to write 'an expression of the American mind.' In fact, the idea of all men (let alone women) being created equal was still way ahead of the average American mind.

This means rights that cannot be removed.

We hold these truths to be self-evident, that all men are created equal, that they are endowed by their Creator with certain **unalienable rights**, that among these are life, liberty and the pursuit of happiness. That to secure these rights, governments are **instituted** among men, deriving their just powers from the consent of the governed. That whenever any form of government becomes destructive to these ends, it is the right of the people to alter or to abolish it, and to institute new government.

Instituted means 'set up'.

The introduction to Thomas Paine's *Common Sense* cleverly lifted the American cause from the specific to the general, making it appear part of a universal struggle for the freedom of people everywhere.

This is an exaggeration – no colony had been so ravaged.

Extirpating means 'removing'.

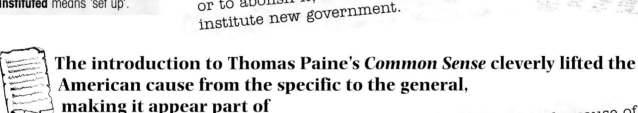

The cause of America is in a great measure the cause of all mankind. Many circumstances have, and will arise, which are not local, but universal, and through which the principles of all lovers of mankind are affected... The laying of a country **desolate with fire and sword**, declaring war against the natural rights of all mankind, and **extirpating** the defenders thereof from the face of the earth, is the concern of every man to whom nature hath given the power of feeling.

THE BUSINESS OF WAR

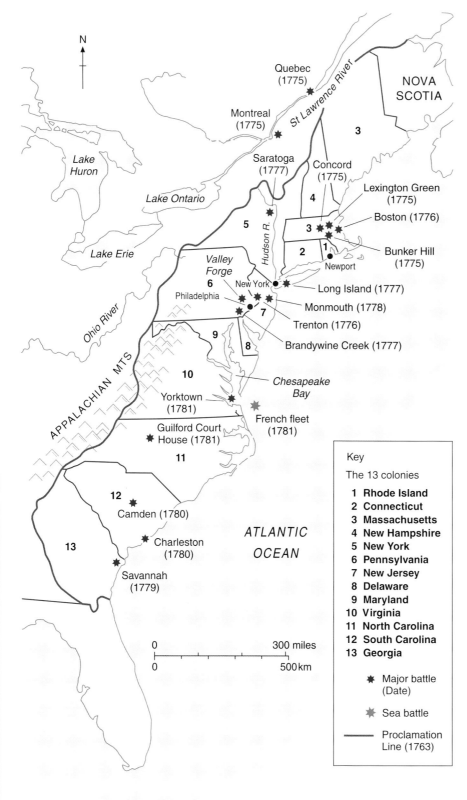

Quebec (1775)

NOVA SCOTIA

Montreal (1775)

St Lawrence River

Lake Huron

Lake Ontario

Saratoga (1777)

Concord (1775)

Lexington Green (1775)

Boston (1776)

Bunker Hill (1775)

Lake Erie

Hudson R.

Newport

Valley Forge

New York

Long Island (1777)

Philadelphia

Monmouth (1778)

Trenton (1776)

Brandywine Creek (1777)

Ohio River

APPALACHIAN MTS

Chesapeake Bay

Yorktown (1781)

French fleet (1781)

Guilford Court House (1781)

Camden (1780)

ATLANTIC OCEAN

Charleston (1780)

Savannah (1779)

0   300 miles
0   500km

Key

The 13 colonies

1 **Rhode Island**
2 **Connecticut**
3 **Massachusetts**
4 **New Hampshire**
5 **New York**
6 **Pennsylvania**
7 **New Jersey**
8 **Delaware**
9 **Maryland**
10 **Virginia**
11 **North Carolina**
12 **South Carolina**
13 **Georgia**

✴ Major battle (Date)

✴ Sea battle

—— Proclamation Line (1763)

THE AMERICAN WAR OF INDEPENDENCE 1775-83

The Revolutionary War was waged by small armies led by normally inefficient (even incompetent) commanders fighting muddled campaigns. Although some 400,000 Americans enlisted in their local militia or the Continental Army (see page 28), they generally served for only a few months. The total in arms at any one time never reached 30,000, and the American commander George Washington could rely on no more than 5000 regular soldiers. Britain's professional army, including many foreign mercenaries (see page 29) was larger but not large enough to subdue the Americans.

The British clung on to Boston until March 1776, when they evacuated the town. In June they suffered another reverse at Charleston, South Carolina. They had better fortune in the north, however, when the Americans failed to take Quebec and called off their invasion of Canada.

Meanwhile, a large British force under the command of General William Howe and his brother Admiral Lord Richard Howe landed on Long Island and drove Washington from New York. After this defeat it looked as if the American cause was lost. But Washington seized the initiative with a daring Christmas raid across the River Delaware that brought him 1000 prisoners and stirred his countrymen to stiffen their resolve.

The campaigns of the following year (1777) changed the course

General Horatio Gates (?1728-1806) reviews the British prisoners that came into his hands after their surrender at Saratoga, October 1777.

THE COST OF WAR

Congress had serious problems paying for the war. Unable to tax, it borrowed about $16 million, collected around $5.5 million from the states, and printed some $240 million in paper notes. These were not backed by gold or silver, and soon became almost worthless. Each state also printed its own (equally worthless) money. As soldiers in the Continental army were paid low wages in useless money, it was remarkable that the army held together at all.

Hardly worth the paper it was printed on: an American $20 bill of 1775

of war. The British planned to split the north from the south and overcome each part in turn. General John Burgoyne advanced slowly from Canada to link up with Howe on the Hudson River. But Howe decided not to wait and moved off by sea to Pennsylvania. He defeated Washington at Brandywine Creek (11 September) and entered Philadelphia, the American capital, a fortnight later. However, it was now too late for Howe to get back to help Burgoyne, who had struggled through to the Hudson. After defeats at the hands of the American generals Benedict Arnold and Horatio Gates, Burgoyne surrendered at Saratoga (17 October). The victory raised hopes on both sides of the Atlantic, and the French, who had been secretly assisting the Americans since 1776, finally committed themselves to full-scale war with Britain.

Washington's army spent the severe winter of 1777-8 camped at Valley Forge, a commanding height on the road north from Philadelphia. The men endured terrible deprivation, as this extract from the colourful diary of the army surgeon Albigence Waldo relates. Nevertheless, Washington used the time to discipline and train his recruits into an effective fighting force.

Fatigues means 'tiredness'.   **Alacrity** means 'alertness'.

December 14. The Army... now begins to grow sickly from the continued fatigues they have suffered this campaign. Yet they still show a spirit of alacrity and contentment not to be expected from so young troops. I am sick – discontented – and out of humour. Poor food – hard lodging – cold weather – fatigue – nasty clothes – nasty cookery – vomit half my time – smoked out my senses – the Devil's in it! I can't endure it! Why are we sent here to starve and freeze? What sweet felicities have I left at home! A charming wife – pretty children – good beds – good food – good cookery – all agreeable – all harmonious. Here all confusion...

Felicities means 'joys'.   This means 'in a bad mood'.

ALLIES

In many ways it better suited the French to continue helping the American rebels secretly (for example, France was America's chief source of gunpowder) rather than making a formal alliance. It was not long since the Seven Years' War when France had been at war with the American colonials. Moreover, France itself was a colonial power and hardly keen to promote rebellion in its own colonies.

Nevertheless, the prospect of avenging the humiliation of 1763 proved too tempting. Guided by the skilful diplomacy of Benjamin Franklin, representatives of the American and French governments signed pacts of alliance on 6 February 1778.

The British Prime Minister Lord North had foreseen what might happen after Saratoga (see page 33). In an effort to bring the war to a swift conclusion before Britain's European enemies became involved, he proposed that America become a self-governing state within the British

The British warship *Royal William*, in about 1757. Although the Royal Navy was very powerful, during the Revolutionary War it was stretched beyond its capabilities.

Empire. The Americans might have accepted such an idea before the fighting broke out. But now they were an independent nation at war, and North's proposal fell on deaf ears.

The entry of France into the war added enormously to Britain's difficulties. The French attacked Britain's colonies in the Caribbean and elsewhere, and harassed its shipping in the Atlantic. The appearance of a powerful French fleet in American waters stretched

the Royal Navy to its limits. Spain joined the anti-British coalition in July 1779, and the United Provinces (the Netherlands) in December 1780. Russia, Sweden and Denmark formed an Armed Neutrality (1780), pledging to use force to stop the Royal Navy interfering with their trade with its enemies. As a result, Britain lost control of the seas for the first time that century.

The French seized the Mediterranean island of Minorca, besieged Gibraltar and took a number of Caribbean islands. At one time a joint invasion by France and Spain of Britain itself was contemplated. In such circumstances, it became ever more difficult for Britain to reinforce and supply its forces in America.

If Britain was going to win the war, a decisive victory early in

The Battle of Monmouth Court House, at which Washington's army showed a new-found professionalism

1778 was essential. General Howe missed this opportunity when he failed to strike at Washington's weakened army at Valley Forge in Pennsylvania (see page 33). In May, General Henry Clinton replaced Howe and set out for New York. Washington's army, rested, reinforced and reorganised, attacked Clinton at Monmouth Court House, New Jersey, on 28 June. Although neither side won a clear victory, the Americans displayed a new discipline and courage. The British now abandoned hope of victory in the north and turned their attentions to the colonies in the south.

THE FIRST AMERICAN DIPLOMATS

The spy-story antics (for example, writing in invisible ink) of Congress' first emissaries to France, Silas Deane and Arthur Lee, only made America's diplomacy look foolish. In December 1776, the situation was transformed by the arrival of the world-famous scientist Benjamin Franklin. He used his experience of European society to win French hearts by acting the part of an unsophisticated pioneer. His charm and diplomacy helped forge the Franco-American alliance, and he remained the United States' minister in Paris until 1785.

A meeting of two worlds: Benjamin Franklin is presented to the king of France, 1776.

The Franco-American alliance of February 1778 was in theory defensive, intended to protect the United States. However, both parties knew only too well that the French would use the war to attack British colonies elsewhere.

ARTICLE 2
The essential and direct end of the present defensive alliance is to maintain effectually the liberty, sovereignty, and independence absolute and unlimited of the said United States, as well in matters of government as of commerce.

France did not officially declare war on Britain until later in the year.

This means 'in government and commercial matters'.

Captain Alexander Graydon, remembering the enormous problems he had recruiting men for his company in 1776, dispels the myth that all Americans were bent on 'Liberty or Death'.

Enlist means 'join the army'.

A number of fellows at the tavern [in Frankford]... indicated a desire to enlist, but although they drank freely of our liquor, they still held off. I soon perceived that the object was to amuse themselves at our expense... One fellow... began to grow insolent... At length the... ruffian... squared himself for battle and advanced towards me... Taking excellent aim, I struck him with the utmost force between the eyes and sent him staggering to the other end of the room... This incident would be little worthy of relating, did it not serve in some degree to correct the error of those who seem to conceive the year 1776 to have been a season of almost universal patriotic enthusiasm.

YORKTOWN

It took a while for the full impact of the French alliance to be felt. In the meantime, American commanders continued to suffer from the problems that had plagued them all along – desertions, defections and mutinies resulting from poor provisions, confused terms of enlistment (soldiers were unsure for how long they were expected to serve) and dreadful pay.

In these circumstances it looked for a time as if the British campaign to overcome the southern colonies might succeed. While Clinton (see page 35) remained at his base in New York, in autumn 1778 General Archibald Campbell carried out a successful seaborne invasion of Georgia, took Savannah and soon controlled the whole state.

Clinton himself then took command and on 12 May 1780 captured Charleston, the most important city in the south. About 5000 American soldiers, including three generals, were captured. Then, fearing a French attack on Newport, Rhode Island, Clinton returned to New York. He left 8000 men in Charleston under the command of General Charles Cornwallis.

Buoyed by recent success, Cornwallis struck north and in August smashed the army of General Gates at Camden, South Carolina. Advancing into North Carolina, at Guilford Court House he met stiffer resistance from a new American commander Nathaniel Greene (15 March 1781) before moving on to Virginia. Here Cornwallis began building up a base at Yorktown, from where he expected to be supplied from the sea. Meanwhile, the Americans had recovered their position in South Carolina and contained the remaining British forces in Charleston and Savannah.

By late summer, Cornwallis' position was deteriorating fast.

A French artist's impression of American and French generals co-operating during the siege of Yorktown, 1781.

While American forces prevented his moving inland, a large French fleet carrying 3000 troops under the command of the Count de Grasse was sailing up from the West Indies to join the siege. In September, Washington moved south from New York with his army. The fate of Cornwallis was sealed when de Grasse overcame the local British fleet in Chesapeake Bay (5 September). Washington arrived at Yorktown three weeks later. On 19 October, Cornwallis surrendered his entire army of 7000 men. As they handed over their weapons, the band reportedly played 'The World Turned Upside Down'.

The French naval victory off the Virginia Capes (Chesapeake Bay) in September 1781 ended any hope that the British garrison in Yorktown could be relieved.

The British grenadier Lieutenant Hale, describing the British advance before Monmouth Court House, gives some insight into the terrible conditions endured by 18th-century soldiers.

Five miles equals eight km.

Procured means 'got hold of'.

Expired means 'died'.

We proceeded five miles in a road composed of nothing but sand which scorched through our shoes with intolerable heat; the sun beating on our heads with a force scarcely to be conceived in Europe, and not a drop of water to assuage our parching thirst. A number of soldiers were unable to support the fatigue, and died on the spot. A corporal who had by some means procured water, drank to such excess as to burst and expired in the utmost torments. Two became raving mad, and the whole road, strewed with miserable wretches wishing for death, exhibited the most shocking scene I ever saw.

The Articles of Capitulation accepted by Cornwallis at Yorktown specified precisely how the humiliating surrender was to be conducted.

This means Yorktown.

This means 'flags rolled up'.

Article III... The garrison of York will march out to a place to be appointed in front of the posts, at two o'clock precisely, with shouldered arms, colours cased, and drums beating a British or German march. They are then to ground their arms, and return to their encampments, where they will remain until they are despatched to the places of their destination.

RATIFICATION

The authors of the new Constitution laid down that it would come into effect only when accepted by at least nine states. A state's opinion was to be decided by an elected meeting, or convention. This contradicted the Articles of Confederation, in which it was stated that they could be altered only by a unanimous vote of all the states. The new Constitution's authors got round this by saying their plan did not alter the Articles but replaced them by popular consent.

Many people who opposed ratification, known as 'Antifederalists', were suspicious of these arrangements. They mistrusted the delegates who had written the Constitution. In particular, many Westerners were wary of the manner in which a group of wealthy intellectuals had drawn it up in secret (see page 44). Many Antifederalists were concerned

Once Britain's restriction on westward expansion had been removed, American pioneers began pouring over the Appalachian Mountains to settle on the rich farmlands beyond.

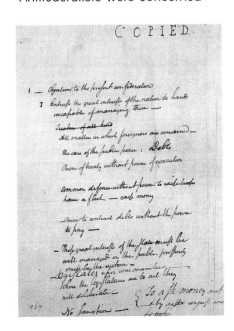

A page from Alexander Hamilton's notes, made for a vital speech given at the Constitutional convention in 1787.

that a powerful presidency might turn into a new monarchy. Others feared that federal institutions would overwhelm the states and ruin local economies. The absence of a Bill of Rights to protect individuals was another cause of concern.

Aware of the opposition, the pro-constitution Federalists launched a massive propaganda campaign. Washington and Franklin supported the campaign, but the major contribution came in the form of 85 essays

(collectively known as *The Federalist Papers*) written by Hamilton, Madison and John Jay under the pseudonym 'Publius' ('In the name of the people').

Delaware's convention accepted the Constitution first (7 December 1787), followed five days later by Pennsylvania. New Jersey's acceptance came before Christmas and Georgia's on 2 January. A week later Connecticut brought the number of states in favour to five. When a Bill of Rights was proposed as a constitutional amendment, Massachusetts, Maryland, South Carolina and New Hampshire raised the total to nine.

Although the required majority had now been reached, New York and Virginia had yet to decide. Because of their wealthy and large populations, the United States would have found it difficult to survive without them. The battle to get them on board was long and hard fought. Eventually, in late June, the Federalists triumphed in Virginia's convention by 89 votes to 79 and in New York's by 30 votes to 27. North Carolina joined in November and Rhode Island in May 1790.

THE FEDERALIST PAPERS

The Federalist Papers appeared as a series of articles in New York newspapers. Although written to support the Federalist cause and urge New Yorkers to ratify the new constitution, they went much further. The authors – Hamilton, Madison and Jay – discussed a wide range of political issues and in doing so produced the most valuable contribution to political thought ever to come out of America (see document page 51).

 A letter by 'Philadelphiensis' (published in the *Antifederalist*, 1788) played on fears that the US President would be even more powerful and dangerous than George III had been.

... the president is a king to all intents and purposes, and at the same time one of the most dangerous kind too – an elective king, the commander-in-chief of a standing army, etc. and to add, that he has a **negative** over the proceedings of both branches of the legislature: and to complete his uncontrolled sway, he is neither restrained nor assisted by a privy council, which is a novelty in government. I challenge the politicians of the whole continent to find in any period of history a monarch more absolute.

A **negative** means the power to stop legislation – a veto.

Speaking in the Massachusetts Convention, Patrick Henry produced one of the most powerful attacks on the new Constitution. He began by questioning the basis of its popular authority.

Have they said, 'We the States'? Have they made a proposal of a compact between states? If they had, this would be a confederation. It is otherwise most clearly a consolidated government. The question turns, sir, on that poor little thing – the expression, 'We, the people,' instead of 'the states' of America. I need not make much pains to show that the principles of this system are extremely pernicious, impolitic, and dangerous.

This means a unitary or non-confederate government.

Patrick Henry (1736-99) was the revolutionary statesman from Virginia who opposed ratification of the Constitution and put forward the Bill of Rights as a safeguard of individual and states' rights.

PAPER INTO PRACTICE

George Washington was the obvious choice as the United States' first president.

Early in 1789, states began to elect representatives for the House of Representatives and the Senate. Both houses opened in New York in April 1789 (the government moved to a purpose-built capital city between Maryland and Virginia, Washington D.C., in 1800).

Representatives and Senators were elected by voters in each state. The president, however, was indirectly elected: the states voted for members of an electoral college which then chose the president. The first president of the United States was George Washington, with John Adams his vice-president. After making a triumphant journey from Virginia to New York, Washington set about establishing the executive.

Meanwhile, Congress was filling in the gaps left by the Constitution. It created an attorney general (the chief law officer who represented the government in the law courts) and other federal posts. The 1789 Judiciary Act set up a judicial structure of 13 federal courts, three appeal courts and a supreme court.

Several states had refused to ratify the Constitution without the promise of a Bill of Rights. Consequently, Madison drew up 12 key rights and put them

forward as constitutional amendments. By 1791, 10 of these rights had been ratified by the necessary three-quarters of the states. The Bill of Rights limited the powers of the federal government to those outlined in the Constitution. It also guaranteed certain fundamental rights such as freedom of speech, religion and assembly, and the right to bear arms.

The American Revolution was now complete. In the space of less than 30 years, the 13 British colonies in North America had come to realise that they had more in common with each other than with Britain, and had bound themselves together in a unique republican union. But neither the Americans nor anyone else foresaw at the time that the creation of the United States of America would alter the course of world history for ever.

In the late 18th century the city of New York was already a cosmopolitan hive of business and enterprise.

PRESIDENT WASHINGTON

In many ways George Washington was the ideal choice as America's first president. He did not want the president to become a new-style king and took great care to stick closely to the letter of the Constitution. At the same time, his personal lifestyle gave the office both respect and dignity. He lived in a Manhattan mansion, travelled in a grand coach and employed almost two dozen servants. A good administrator, he wanted the USA to be governed by the most able people, whatever their viewpoint. He was disappointed, therefore, when political parties emerged in the 1790s (see page 52), and retired to his Virginia home in 1797.

George Washington in retirement, talking with African American workers on his country estate.

The first Amendment to the US Constitution combined several rights previously contained in state bills of rights. The Second Amendment, accepted without a murmur at the time, is today one of the most controversial.

This did not stop a state from having an established church.

This means 'dealing with their complaints'.

I. Congress shall make no law respecting an **establishment of religion**, or prohibiting the free exercise thereof; or abridging the freedom of speech, or of the press; or the right of the people peaceably to assemble, and to petition the government for **a redress of grievances**.
II. A well regulated militia, being necessary to the security of a free state, the right of the people to keep and bear arms, shall not be infringed.

In *The Federalist* paper no. 67 Hamilton complained bitterly at the way the powers proposed for the president in the Constitution had been grossly misrepresented by Antifederalists (see page 48).

Scrupled means 'hesitated'.

Apprehensions means 'worries'.

This refers to the supposed similarity between the president and a monarch.

An executive officer, here the president.

Prerogatives means 'powers'.

Calculating upon the aversion of the people to monarchy, [writers against the constitution]... have endeavored to enlist all their jealousies and **apprehensions** in opposition to the intended President of the United States... To establish the **pretended affinity**, they have not **scrupled** to draw resources even from the regions of fiction. The authorities of a **magistrate**, in few instances greater, in some instances less, than those of a governor of New York, have been magnified into more than royal **prerogatives**.

THE IMPACT OF THE REVOLUTION
PARTIES AND POWER

The changes of 1765-91 had an impact on every aspect of American life. Most obviously, the tie with Britain was cut and the USA was established. Secondly, an enduring framework of government was set up. Thirdly, the USA was free to expand westwards and exploit its vast economic potential (see map). Nevertheless, two important developments remained before the new system could operate

effectively: political parties and a means of interpreting the Constitution.

The Constitution made no mention of political parties, which were commonly associated with corruption and self-interest. Nevertheless, parties emerged in the 1790s. The Democratic Republicans formed around Jefferson, who stood for the rights of the states, individual liberty and agriculture. The

Thomas Jefferson (1743-1826), third president of the United States and leader of the Democratic Republicans.

THE WESTWARD EXPANSION OF THE USA

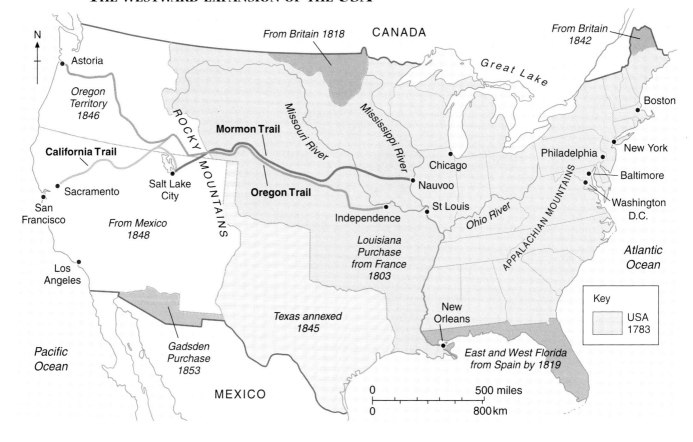

conservative Federalists, inspired by Hamilton and John Adams and drawing their support from the towns and wealthy classes, wished to build up the power of the national (or federal) government. By 1796 parties were operating in Congress and organised the Jefferson v. Adams presidential election, which Adams won. From this time forward, the party system was a key feature of most American politics.

Although the Constitution was the basis of government, its wording needed practical interpretation. For example, what did Article I, Section 8 (1) mean when it gave Congress taxing and spending powers for the 'general welfare of the United States'?

Working on the premise that the Constitution was the highest law of the land, the right to interpret it was claimed by the federal courts. This principle was brilliantly set out in Chief Justice John Marshall's ruling in the Marbury v. Madison case (1803) (see document). This development gave the Supreme Court huge power to influence American life. For example, Amendment XIV (1868) tried to protect African Americans by granting civil rights to 'All persons born or naturalised in the United States'. The 1875 Civil Rights Act attempted to put this into practice. However, in 1883 the Supreme Court said the Act was invalid. This undermined Amendment XIV and African Americans were not guaranteed full civil rights until the 20th century.

1875 CIVIL RIGHTS ACT

One hundred years after the Declaration of Independence, Congress passed a Civil Rights Act to give all citizens – whatever their 'nativity [birth], race, colour, or persuasion, religious or political – the right to use inns, public transport, theatres and places of public amusement'. This was an attempt to end discrimination against non-whites. However, the Supreme Court ruled that the Act was not based on Amendment XIV and was therefore unconstitutional, because it sought to protect rights that were social, and not civil.

 A key principle of American political life, the right of the federal courts to interpret the Constitution (known as Judicial Review), was established by Chief Justice John Marshall. His famous ruling in the Marbury v. Madison case made the Supreme Court 'the umpire of the Constitution'.

Expound means 'explain'.

It is emphatically the province and duty of the judicial department to say what the law is. Those who apply the rule to particular cases must of necessity expound and interpret that rule. If two laws conflict with each other, the courts must decide on the operation of each. So if a law be in opposition to the constitution; if both the law and the constitution apply to a particular case... The court must determine which of these conflicting rules governs the case. That is the very essence of the judicial duty.

John Marshall (1755-1835)

WHOSE REVOLUTION?

The states allowed only adult males to vote in federal elections. In every state apart from Vermont, the franchise (right to vote) was further limited by wealth or property qualifications. Consequently, in 1789 only about 25 percent of adult males had the vote. Virtually all women and non-whites were excluded.

That said, the Constitution's first three words – 'We, the people' – seemed to promise equality under the Constitution for all Americans. It took more than two centuries for the promise to be fulfilled. White men benefited first: property qualifications for voters had largely gone by 1840, and ten years later all American adult white males enjoyed the right to vote.

Initially, the Revolution set back female suffrage. By 1807 the states that had allowed women to vote in local elections had withdrawn that right. It was restored in Kentucky in 1834. In 1869 the territory of Wyoming (a state in 1889) granted full female suffrage. Other states followed over the next 50 years, until the 19th Amendment (1919) said voting was not to be restricted on account of sex. However, full civil rights did not come with enfranchisement. Only in the late 20th century were American women beginning to enjoy the civil rights implied by the Revolution.

The Revolution's greatest failing was side-stepping the issue of slavery. Because the economy of the southern states was based upon slave labour,

they would not have joined a Union in which slavery was illegal. So the issue was swept under the carpet until settled by the Civil War (1861-5). Even after the abolition of slavery (1865), discrimination was rife in many areas of American life, especially in the South, until tackled by the Civil Rights movement of the second half of the 20th century.

For Native Americans the Revolution spelled disaster. It removed the British attempt to stop westward expansion, opening up Native American homelands to predatory pioneers. Sporadic fighting, culminating in defeat for Native Americans in the Indian Wars of 1865-80, left them a dispirited people living in pitiful reservations. Although granted American citizenship in

Women voters in New Jersey, in about 1800. Shortly afterwards, women's right to vote was removed – only to be restored later in the century.

The Unionist army captures Atlanta (1864) on the way to victory in the Civil War of 1861-5.

1924, they continued for years to suffer from racial discrimination.

For women and non-white Americans, therefore, the Revolution fell short of its own high expectations. Nonetheless, it gave Americans a vocabulary of rights, liberty and equality which would eventually guide them towards a truly democratic future.

THE LEAGUE OF THE GREAT PEACE

Ironically, democracy and federalism had been practised in America long before the white man arrived. They were key features of the League of the Great Peace, formed in the 16th century or earlier by five Iroquois-speaking nations of Native Americans. The League respected the rights of each nation (state) and gave all people a say in government. Women, the providers of the next generation, were much respected and had the right to make and unmake chiefs. White men studied the League's customs, which influenced the form of the government of the United States.

Iroquois villages, from a mid 17th-century map

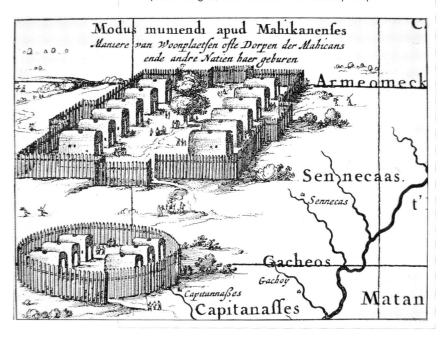

This extract comes from an address written by Jupiter Harmon, a slave living on Long Island, New York, to his fellow African Americans in 1787. The writing gives some insight into the disappointment African Americans felt at being excluded from the benefits of the revolution.

This means 'so busy trying for'.

Late means 'recent'.

That liberty is a great thing we may know from our own feelings, and we may likewise judge so from the conduct of the white people in the late war. How much money has been spent and how many lives have been lost to defend their liberty? I must say that I have hoped that God would open their eyes, when they were so much engaged for liberty, to think of the state of the poor blacks, and to pity us.

VIVE LA LIBERTÉ...!

France was involved in most stages of the American Revolution. Its war with Britain had led to the Stamp Act and the colonial tax revolt. The ideas of the European Enlightenment, many coming from France, inspired Americans in their quest for natural rights. And when war came, French forces played a crucial role in American victory.

Meanwhile, American ideas and influences swept back across the Atlantic Ocean. Wealthier members of the French middle class, obsessed with a romantic notion of America as a haven of liberty inhabited by noble farmers, adorned their mansions with engravings of American scenes. 'Republic' and 'liberty' became the words of the moment.

On a political level, the participation in the American War of Independence brought the French monarchy to crisis

point. The royal government spent a staggering 1.3 billion livres (more than twice its annual income) helping the Americans to defeat the British. Most of it was raised not in taxation but in loans it could not hope to repay. The result was financial disaster.

The revolution in France began in 1789. The citizens of Paris, many poor and starving, stormed the Bastille, a royal fortress-prison. The revolution spread throughout the country. An elected National Assembly (like a Congress or parliament) began reforming the country's old-fashioned government and traditions. In 1792, France removed King Louis XVI from power and became a republic, like America.

Several French opposition leaders drew their inspiration from America. If Americans had improved their lot through revolution, why not the French? The Marquis of Lafayette, who had fought with Washington (after whom he named his eldest son),

The Marquis of Lafayette (1757-1834), the French revolutionary leader who learned his republican principles in America, where he fought with George Washington

French revolutionaries install a Liberty Tree of their own (about 1789).

was just such an idealist. The declaration of rights he presented to the French National Assembly was unashamedly based upon the American Declaration of Independence. Later, horrified by revolutionary excesses (see box), Lafayette fled the country.

As Lafayette discovered, the two revolutions shared the same vocabulary, but little else. America's revolution was about national independence and focused on a common enemy – the British. France's revolution began with the disintegration of a regime and developed into a chaotic power struggle between classes and other groups.

AMERICAN REACTIONS

In 1789, Americans reacted with delight to the news that the French had followed their example and risen up against their king. Four years later the leadership of the revolution passed into the hands of radicals who executed Louis XVI and instituted a bloody 'reign of terror'. Some Americans, including Washington, recoiled in horror at this assault on religion, property and authority. Others, headed by Jefferson, condemned French violence but continued to support what they believed was the cause of freedom.

The aristocratic Vicomtesse de Fars-Fausselandry remembered how passionately she and her friends had supported the American Revolution. They did not consider that its principles ran contrary to their own privileged position.

The American cause seemed our own; we were proud of their victories, we cried at their defeats, we tore down bulletins and read them in out houses. None of us reflected on the danger that the New World could give to the old.

Like many Americans, Thomas Paine (see pages 30-1) welcomed the outbreak of the French Revolution. In a preface to *The Rights of Man* (1791-2), he hoped that it would spread to England. But events in France became too hot even for Paine. In 1794 he was arrested as a moderate and released only because he was an American citizen.

This British cartoon of Thomas Paine reflects the widespread disillusionment with revolutionary principles that followed the French Revolution's descent into carnage by 1793.

The cause of the French people is that of all Europe, or rather of the whole world; but the governments of all those countries are by no means favourable to it... There ought not now to exist any doubt that the peoples of France, England, and America, enlightened and enlightening each other, shall henceforth be able, not merely to give the world an example of good government, but by their united influence enforce its practice.

THE POST-WAR WORLD

The storming of the Bastille in Paris (see page 56) captured the popular imagination in a way that the measured pronouncements of the Second Continental Congress in America never did. The immediate impact of the French Revolution was greater, too, because it promised so much to so many. It became the pattern for other violent revolutions – from the uprising against the Spaniards in Argentina (1816) to the Russian Revolution in St Petersburg in 1917.

The long-term impact of the American Revolution was more subtle and more enduring. It taught through example, not force. It gave the world the belief that nations have the right to determine their own future. This concept lay at the heart of the Fourteen Points that President Wilson offered as the basis for a peace settlement after World War I (see page 59).

The legacy of the American Revolution for colonial powers was obvious. During the 19th and 20th centuries, Britain eventually bowed to the inevitable and granted its colonies their independence. Most other imperial powers did the same.

The impact of the American Constitution and its style of government has also been considerable. A written constitution, first used in the USA, is now common throughout the world. Many countries, from Canada (1841), to Australia (1901) and Germany (1949), use a form of federalism. The rule of law, checks and balances, and the separation of powers are widely recognised as essential to democratic government.

Perhaps the most powerful of all the legacies of the American Revolution has been its concept of individual freedom. It is not a government-led freedom from hunger or poverty, for example. But it is the freedom to do things such as speak, worship, assemble, publish and make money. It is this, more than anything else, that has drawn millions of people across the oceans to join the extraordinarily successful phenomenon that is the United States of America.

Welcome to a new world: Italian immigrants arriving at Ellis Island, New York, in about 1905

In January 1918 President Wilson presented Congress with his Fourteen Points for the establishment of world peace. The principle of national self-determination featured in many of them.

A European empire that collapsed in 1918.

Autonomous means 'independent'.

A European-Middle Eastern empire that collapsed in 1918.

This means 'free from interference'.

5. [We want] A free, open-minded, and absolutely impartial adjustment of all colonial claims... [in which] the interests of the populations concerned must have equal weight ...

10. The peoples of Austria-Hungary... should be accorded the freest opportunity of autonomous development.

12. The Turkish portions of the present Ottoman empire should be assured a secure sovereignty, but the other nationalities... should be assured an absolutely unmolested opportunity of autonomous development.

Program for the Peace of the World
By PRESIDENT WILSON January 8, 1918

I. Open covenants of peace, openly arrived at, after which there shall be no private international understandings of any kind, but diplomacy shall proceed always frankly and in the public view.

II. Absolute freedom of navigation upon the seas, outside territorial waters, alike in peace and in war, except as the seas may be closed in whole or in part by international action for the enforcement of international covenants.

III. The removal, so far as possible, of all economic barriers and the establishment of an equality of trade conditions among all the nations consenting to the peace and associating themselves for its maintenance.

IV. Adequate guarantees given and taken that national armaments will reduce to the lowest point consistent with domestic safety.

V. Free, open-minded, and absolutely impartial adjustment of all colonial claims, based upon a strict observance of the principle that in determining all such questions of sovereignty the interests of the population concerned must have equal weight with the equitable claims of the government whose title is to be determined.

VI. The evacuation of all Russian territory and such a settlement of all questions affecting Russia as will secure the best and freest coöperation of the other nations of the world in obtaining for her an unhampered and unembarrassed opportunity for the independent determination of her own political development and national policy, and assure her of a sincere welcome into the society of free nations under institutions of her own choosing; and, more than a welcome, assistance also of every kind that she may need and may herself desire. The treatment accorded Russia by her sister nations in the months to come will be the acid test of their goodwill, of their comprehension of her needs as distinguished from their own interests, and of their intelligent and unselfish sympathy.

VII. Belgium, the whole world will agree, must be evacuated and restored, without any attempt to limit the sovereignty which she enjoys in common with all other free nations. No other single act will serve as this will serve to restore confidence among the nations in the law which they have themselves set and determined for the government of their relations with one another. Without this healing act the whole structure and validity of international law is forever impaired.

VIII. All French territory should be freed and the invaded portions restored, and the wrong done to France by Prussia in 1871 in the matter of Alsace-Lorraine, which has unsettled the peace of the world for nearly fifty years, should be righted, in order that peace may once more be made secure in the interest of all.

IX. A readjustment of the frontiers of Italy should be effected along clearly recognizable lines of nationality.

X. The people of Austria-Hungary, whose place among the nations we wish to see safeguarded and assured, should be accorded the freest opportunity of autonomous development.

XI. Rumania, Serbia and Montenegro should be evacuated; occupied territories restored; Serbia accorded free and secure access to the sea; and the relations of the several Balkan States to one another determined by friendly counsel along historically established lines of allegiance and nationality; and international guarantees of the political and economic independence and territorial integrity of the several Balkan States should be entered into.

XII. The Turkish portions of the present Ottoman Empire should be assured a secure sovereignty, but the other nationalities which are now under Turkish rule should be assured an undoubted security of life and an absolutely unmolested opportunity of autonomous development, and the Dardanelles should be permanently opened as a free passage to the ships and commerce of all nations under international guarantees.

XIII. An independent Polish State should be erected which should include the territories inhabited by indisputably Polish populations, which should be assured a free and secure access to the sea, and whose political and economic independence and territorial integrity should be guaranteed by international covenant.

XIV. A general association of nations must be formed under specific covenants for the purpose of affording mutual guarantees of political independence and territorial integrity to great and small States alike.

In March 1947 President Truman outlined a doctrine that, for the first time, pledged practical support for the principles of the American Revolution in other countries.

President Harry S. Truman (1884-1973)

At the present moment in world history nearly every nation must choose between alternative ways of life... One way... is based upon the will of the majority, and is distinguished by free institutions, representative government, free elections, guarantees of individual liberty, freedom of speech and religion, and freedom from political oppression.
The second way... is based upon the will of a minority forcibly imposed upon the majority. It relies upon terror and oppression... and the suppression of personal freedoms.
I believe that it must be the policy of the United States to support free peoples... primarily through economic and financial aid.

GLOSSARY

Admiralty The British government department responsible for the Royal Navy.

Antifederalists Those Americans who campaigned against ratification of the 1787 constitution. They believed it gave the president too much power and undermined the independence of the states.

Archbishop of Canterbury The appointed head of the episcopal Church of England.

Bill of Rights A legally binding declaration of people's civil liberties or rights. The British Bill of Rights was passed by parliament in 1689. The American Bill of Rights was set out in the first 10 amendments to the Constitution (1791).

boycott A widespread refusal to participate in or buy something. In the lead up to the Revolution, the Americans frequently boycotted British goods.

cash crop A crop, such as tobacco, that is grown to be sold for money rather than personal use.

Chancellor of the Exchequer The British minister responsible for financial affairs.

Charles I The king of England (reigned 1642-9) who fought a Civil War, lost and was executed. For the next 11 years Britain was a republic.

checks and balances A scheme for limiting the power of different branches of government by dividing powers and duties between them.

commissioner A servant of the king given a specific task.

confederation A loose alliance of states in which supreme authority is retained by the states and not in a central government.

Congress A large meeting or assembly of delegates from several states. The name was chosen for the parliament of the United States.

constitution The laws and conventions by which a country is governed.

Continental Congress A congress of all the American colonies (later states).

Crown (the) The British government, which nominally operated on behalf of the king or queen.

delegates Emissaries from the states to a congress. Unlike representatives, who were charged with deciding matters for themselves, delegates could fulfil only the wishes and instructions of those who had sent them.

democracy A form of government, famously defined by American President Abraham Lincoln as 'government of the people, by the people, and for the people'.

dissenters Protestants who rejected the Church of England.

East India Company The powerful British company that had a monopoly of trade with India and the Far East.

English Civil War The war (1642-5) fought between Charles I and Parliament over religion and parliamentary rights.

Enlightenment An 18th-century intellectual movement. It attacked all practices, especially religious and political ones, that could not be justified by reason.

executive That part of the government, in the USA headed by the president, that is responsible for executing (carrying out) laws. This means running the day-to-day government, including maintaining law and order, managing the economy and conducting foreign affairs.

Federalism The system that divides government between a central authority and localities, giving substantial powers to each.

Federalists Those Americans who campaigned for ratification of the 1787 Constitution.

garrison Soldiers responsible for defending a town or fortress.

Glorious Revolution The British parliament's removal of King James II (James VII of Scotland), replacing him with the joint rule of Queen Mary II and King William III (1688-9). It marked the final triumph of Parliament over the monarch.

judiciary The branch of government, consisting of courts and judges, concerned with interpreting and enforcing the law.

legislature The branch of government concerned with making law and voting taxation.

Liberty Tree This was a tree (or pole) before which the Sons of Liberty met and promised themselves to the cause of liberty. The first was an elm tree in Boston. Liberty trees soon became symbols of the American cause.

Loyalists Americans who opposed the break with Britain. Also known as 'Tories'.

Members of Parliament (MPs) Members of the British House of Commons.

mercenaries Hired soldiers prepared to join any army as long as they are paid.

militia The American states' local volunteer forces.

molasses A treacle that drains from sugar when it is refined.

natural law Fundamental law that comes from 'nature' – it is not man-made.

Navigation Acts Laws that protected a country's trade by stipulating that it has to pass through home ports, be carried in its own ships, etc.

New England The north-eastern colonies that were originally settled by Puritan refugees.

'New World' A European name for the Americas. Europe and the Middle East were known as the 'Old World'.

nonimportation The American campaign to refuse to accept any goods imported from Britain.

ordinance A law passed by the Second Continental Congress.

Parliament The British representative assembly made up of the elected House of Commons and the non-elected House of Lords. The Commons represented mainly the wealthy while the Lords was made up entirely of nobles.

Patriots Americans who resisted the efforts of the British government to tax the colonies and eventually led the colonies into war.

Prime Minister The chief minister in the British government. Although appointed by the crown, he had to have the support of a majority of MPs.

proclamation A royal decree.

Puritan Someone who wished to 'purify' the Church of England of its Roman Catholic features, such as bishops. More generally, 'puritan' came to mean a strict (and often intolerant) Protestant.

Quaker A member of a Protestant religious group known as the Friends of Truth (later the Religious Society of Friends). Rejecting formal services and professional priests, they believed in each individual being guided by an 'inner light'. The nickname 'Quaker' arose because the group's British founder, George Fox, told a judge to quake at the name of the Lord.

quartering Forcing civilians to host and support troops.

radical Someone who calls for total change, plucking up the existing order by the roots.

ratify To accept officially. The American Constitution had to be ratified by nine of the 13 states before it could become law.

representative A person who, by making their own choices and judgements, reflects the views of those who have sent him or her. Members of the US Congress, like British MPs, are representatives rather than delegates.

Republic A state without a monarch.

Republican government In America, government through the people's representatives rather than direct democracy. The British use the term 'representative government'.

revenue Government income.

Royal Navy The British navy. Between about 1700 and the beginning of the 20th century it was the largest and most powerful in the world.

search warrant A document that gives permission for a search to be made of private property.

self-determination The right of a nation to decide for itself by whom and how it should be governed.

separation of powers The division of government power and duties between the executive, legislature and judiciary. It was a fundamental principle of the American Constitution of 1787.

Sons of Liberty A group of American radicals, led by Samuel Adams and Patrick Henry, founded in 1765 to oppose the Stamp Act. The name was coined by a pro-American British MP.

standing army An army that remains intact in peacetime. The British hatred and distrust of standing armies (which they associated with European tyranny) was shared in the American colonies.

tariff A duty charged on imports.

Tories Another name for the 'loyalists'. The name was originally applied to a conservative British political party of the 17th century.

tyranny A government that acts in its own interest rather than that of the people it governs.

virtual representation The idea that Americans, although they did not elect their own MPs to the House of Commons, were 'virtually' represented there in the same way as British people who did not have the vote.

Whig The more liberal of the two British political parties in the 18th century.

INDEX